EATING WELL

MB MACAW BOOKS

© Macaw Books

www.macawbooks.com

Printed in India

There was once a little boy called Timmy. He wanted to eat only chocolates and chips all day.

Whenever he saw any vegetables, he would say, 'Yuck!' Nothing could make him eat even a bite of a vegetable.

If Mummy gave him any vegetables for breakfast, he would not touch it. Sometimes, he threw his broccoli into the sink.

He never ate any dairy products either. His milk remained untouched until it turned sour and started to smell.

When Mummy gave him apples to eat, Timmy would say, 'No!' If Mummy gave him peas, he said, 'Never!'

Timmy even turned down large, juicy steak! Often Timmy's meals only consisted of slices of cake.

Timmy wasted everything on his dinner plate. He threw all the healthy food in the bin.

As Timmy never ate any fruits and vegetables, his health became poor. His teeth became weak. And then one day, one of his teeth fell in!

All the junk food he ate had made Timmy very weak.
He started to have terrible stomach aches.
Timmy could not even go out to play! All he did was
lie in bed the whole day.

Slowly, Timmy became thin as a stick. He always had a bad cold. His eyesight became very poor.

Timmy understood that he was harming himself by eating only junk food. Now he wished he had listened to his parents.

Suddenly, Timmy began to eat his beans and bread. He stopped eating chocolates and chips.

'From now on, I shall eat only healthy food!' said Timmy. He began to eat all the fruits and vegetables that he could get. Timmy's health started to get better again.

The more healthy food Timmy ate, the stronger he became. He did not fall sick anymore. From then on, Timmy ate only nutritious food and always had the best of health.

MILK, BUTTER AND CHEESE

Will was spending the weekend at his uncle's farm. He was very happy to see the green fields of the farm.

'I cannot wait to eat all the tasty food at the farm!' said Will. He waved at the cows in the meadows as they drove past them.

All the animals at the farm gave different food products. Will was very happy to see all the farm animals.

There were also ten hens, ten ducks and five goats at the farm. Will loved to hear the sound of cows mooing through the day.

Every morning at the farm, Will drank fresh cow milk. He loved that it came straight from the farm cows.

'This is the tastiest milk I have ever had!' said Will, as he gulped down a glass. 'I can feel my bones getting stronger as I drink!'

Will always loved breakfast at the farm. His aunt gave him some freshly baked buns. 'How soft and warm they are!' he said.

The butter at breakfast was freshly churned too. Will loved watching the milkmaid make the butter. Farm butter was so delicious!

Will spread the buns with butter and cheese. The cheese was freshly made from fresh milk too!

Even the honey was freshly collected from the honeybees.
'Mmm! It is so thick and sweet!' said Will.

The eggs too were laid by the hens at the farm. They were delicious and he ate them happily.

After breakfast, Will visited the hen. 'Thank you for your eggs, Mrs. Hen!' he said, earnestly.

Will loved to have pudding at the farm. It was made of fresh cream. He ate his pudding as he walked to meet the cows.

He visited the cows too. 'Thank you for your milk, dear cows!' he said, 'It gave us cheese and butter and cream!'

At the end of the weekend, Will felt much stronger. ´How lucky I am to have such healthy and tasty food to eat!´ he said.